New Design in STITCHERY

New Design in
STITCHERY

Donald J. Willcox

VAN NOSTRAND REINHOLD COMPANY
NEW YORK CINCINNATI TORONTO LONDON MELBOURNE

OTHER BOOKS IN THIS SERIES:

NEW DESIGN IN CERAMICS
NEW DESIGN IN JEWELRY
NEW DESIGN IN WEAVING
NEW DESIGN IN WOOD

Van Nostrand Reinhold Company Regional Offices:
New York   Cincinnati   Chicago   Millbrae   Dallas

Van Nostrand Reinhold Company Foreign Offices:
London   Toronto   Melbourne

Copyright © 1970 by Litton Educational Publishing, Inc.
Library of Congress Catalog Card Number 74-126869

Designed by Myron Hall III
Printed by Halliday Lithograph Corporation
Color printed by Toppan Printing Company, Limited, Japan
Bound by Complete Books Company

Published by Van Nostrand Reinhold Company
450 West 33rd Street, New York, N.Y. 10001

Published simultaneously in Canada by
Van Nostrand Reinhold Ltd.

16   15   14   13   12   11   10   9   8   7   6   5   4   3   2   1

For
KRISTY, JODY, and KIM

CONTENTS

FOREWORD

The illustrations within this volume originate from Scandinavia—Denmark, Norway, Sweden, and Finland. The craftsmen of these countries enjoy a heritage rich in the art of stitchery. By exploring this heritage and the prolific stitchery talents of contemporary Scandinavian craftsmen, it is hoped that this volume will stimulate the curiosity of all stitchery enthusiasts—educators, students, beginning craftsmen, and professionals alike. This book, then, is meant to broaden the reader's horizon in the art of stitchery.

At the back of this book are a list of other books and magazines dealing with Scandinavian stitchery, a list of Scandinavian textile and embroidery schools, and a list of reliable Scandinavian mail-order supply sources, all of which should be helpful to the reader who wishes to explore Scandinavian stitchery further.

WHAT IS STITCHERY?

The word "stitchery" is not a new one in the language of crafts. "To stitch," as everyone probably knows, is to unite thread with other thread or with fabric. But to the modern craftsman, stitchery is much more than just thread techniques—it is a whole new category of experimental designs with thread.

Then isn't stitchery just another term for needlework? Unfortunately, needlework is no longer a valid label for *creative* thread work. It is a tired word and it's fraught with negative connotations. Art educators don't like it because they feel their students regard needlework as a pastime for "the ladies." And too often you hear it used to describe the activities of a sewing circle: pillow covers and tablecloths embroidered to while away idle hours.

A different name has long been needed to revitalize the image of needlecraft—and stitchery is that name. Stitchery is all that is fresh, exciting, and spontaneous in thread work. It is a personal medium for artistic expression, and it's also a craft for everyone, from professional artists to businessmen to women and children.

THREAD Whatever name you employ, one of the essential ingredients of stitchery is and always has been thread. A fairly simple medium, you may think, but not one to be taken for granted. Thread is like potential energy waiting to be used by the stitcher. It has a personality all its own, and that personality will determine the character of the stitchery composition.

What are some of the characteristics of thread? It has texture, it has color, it has dimension, and it casts a shadow. It is affected by light in many ways. Glossy threads of celluloid or metal, for example, will reflect light. So will a hand-spun, natural wool yarn that is heavily coated with lanolin. Hemp, on the other hand, absorbs light, giving a dull or matte finish. Light will pass through a transparent thread of clear plastic, while a partially opaque one—like nylon fish line—will absorb some rays and reflect others, producing translucent effects in a composition.

Threads come in different shapes. Wool yarn is round, leather and plastic threads are usually rectangular. A thread may be very thin, like silk, or thick, like sisal. It may be a single strand or many thin ones twisted together, and its texture will vary according to its contents and also according to the way it has been spun. Wool yarn, for example, is soft and fuzzy, nylon is firm and smooth. Threads spun to the left or right have twists or spirals. Some threads with rather linear-looking textures are actually lengths of unspun filaments.

Most thread is monochromatic, but multicolors are also made. Natural wool yarn, for instance, is sometimes hand-dyed along its length in several colors to give it a candy-cane look. Another method of providing color contrast in thread is to twist two or more strands of different hues together.

Finally, thread is both flexible and firm. It can be manipulated easily and effectively into almost any design, but, because it is *thread,* it is linear, and the patterns it creates will tend to be linear and geometric in character. As I have said, thread is available in endless variety, and many types will be discussed in the section on techniques that follows. For easy reference, here is a list of some variations, both traditional and out-of-the-ordinary, which the craftsman may find useful: linen, sisal, jute, cotton, tar yarn, copper wire, brass wire, string, floss, celluloid, electric cord, bast, tow, mohair, grass, rope, rawhide, root, and bark.

BACKGROUND FABRIC AND OTHER MATERIALS The right background is as important to a stitchery composition as the right thread. This doesn't mean that certain materials are not meant for stitchery, simply that not every fabric is right for every work. And knowing the right one is like knowing thread: it takes curiosity, first of all, then exploration and careful study.

Many craftsmen make it a habit to collect scraps and remnants—bits and pieces of everything for use in their compositions. These materials are available everywhere. Obvious sources are upholstery shops, fabric stores, weaving workshops, and clothing mills. In addition, the stitcher can go to factories and junkyards for scraps of plastic, rubber, and metal; building materials such as fencing, flooring, and screens; glass, nails, machinery parts, and all kinds of industrial discards. He might save fragments of jewelry, odd bits of leather and fur, buttons, feathers, mirrors—just about anything he thinks he might one day have use for. And, of course, nature provides him with some of his most beautiful found objects: leaves, flowers, shells, driftwood, reeds, grass, and stones, to mention only a few.

Obviously there is an enormous variety of materials besides thread just waiting for the creative stitcher. All of these should be explored by him—their personalities probed and their capabilities uncovered. Through constant experimentation with the materials at his disposal, the stitcher will gain the knowledge he needs to select the right ones for a given composition and the discipline he needs to solve problems in design.

TOOLS The basic tool of stitchery is the needle. One of its great advantages is that it's inexpensive, so it doesn't hurt to have a wide variety on hand. Crewel needles are generally used for fine work, chenille needles for medium work, and darning, upholstery, and leather needles, as well as the curved tailoring and sail types, for coarser stitching. Other necessary tools include scissors, wire cutters, and thimbles, as well as a hoop or frame for material that is cumbersome or requires tension. And at some time or other, a designer may also find need for such items as snaps, zippers, buttons, hooks, eyelets, contact cement, paste, glue, and paper for cutting patterns.

The sewing machine is also an important tool for creative stitchery, so don't overlook it just because it's a mechanical device. A regular household machine will meet the demands of most ordinary fabric, but an industrial one, which has both a top and bottom feed, offers much greater flexibility for use with heavy, nontraditional materials. To illustrate, an industrial machine made for use on leather can easily sew through cowhide ⅜ inch thick. There are many fine examples of machine stitchery featured in this text, among them "The Newspaper," an embroidered work by Ann-Mari Kornerup (Figure 14), and "Puzzle," a linen appliqué by Monica Hjelm (Figure 101).

Still another mechanical tool of stitchery is the electric stencil, which will trace a design with tiny holes on pattern paper. The design is then transferred to fabric by rubbing a felt dauber coated with wax dye across the stencil. Electric stencils are used extensively in Scandinavian textile schools; the Danish Handicraft Guild School recommends the Ideal brand, which is distributed in the United States by E. Gatzwiller of Copenhagen. Used industrial sewing machines for classroom or professional use are easily obtained through advertisements in trade magazines.

COLOR A stitcher can use his thread and fabric as is, or he can add color to them before he begins to stitch. One simple method of doing this is *tie-dyeing,* so-called because fabric and thread are tied into knots at regular or random intervals and the knots are dipped into dye. The dye flows unevenly into the knots, producing a rather free-form color pattern in the material. If the process is reversed, and the unknotted sections are dyed, the color flows more evenly into those areas and then "feathers" its way into knots.

Ikat dyeing, a process used in Scandinavia, is a bit more involved. The thread is wound around two posts that project from a 2- or 3-foot-long stick. (Imagine a broom handle with nails sticking out from both ends.) Sections of this thread are then tightly bound with other thread, and the whole stick—thread and all—is dunked in dye solution. The bound sections do not absorb dye, the unbound ones do, and, depending on the way it was bound, an irregular or even pattern results. A variation of this technique is to use wax on those sections of thread or fabric that are to be kept free of color. The wax prevents the dye from soaking in and should not be removed until the material is completely dry.

Vegetable color, aniline dye, leather dye, permanent ink, felt pens, crayon, and paint can all be used to color thread and fabric for stitchery. Several Scandinavians have experimented with a luminous paint that glows in the dark, and craftsmen have also achieved interesting color schemes by silk-screening their background fabrics. Pasting on fragments of photographs, paper cutouts, or bits of fabrics and weaving will add texture as well as color to a composition. Some interesting examples of stitchery collage are the pieces in Figures C-1 and C-3 and in Figure 85.

Color is obviously an aspect of stitchery that is wide open for exploration, and a craftsman who is interested could probably develop all sorts of coloring techniques. At any rate, whether you are experimenting with a new dye or using an already-proven method, it is sound procedure to try it out first on a small scrap of the fabric or thread you intend to use before proceeding with any large-scale coloring of materials.

THE ELEMENTS OF DESIGN

The creative possibilities within stitchery are wide and varied. A piece may be as purely decorative as a wall hanging or as useful as an embroidered handbag. Its design may be abstract, or it may be a landscape, a still life, or a portrait. It may be a composition in negative space—such as the curtains in Figure 138—color, or texture, or any combination of the three. It may have a flat or raised surface; it can even be a free-standing sculpture. The important thing to remember is that stitchery is a separate and unique medium. It is not "painting with thread," as many critics have suggested, because thread is not paint no matter how many similarities you can find between them.

There is nothing haphazard about the composition of a good piece of stitchery. Visually it can be appreciated on several levels, and the craftsman will learn much from examining it in different ways. He can, for example, view it in perspective—take in its forms, colors, and textures, and let it register as a whole. Or he can abstract it in his mind's eye, so that he sees just the lines and curves that suggest form. Or he can go even further, blot out everything recognizable and view it as one vast exercise in texture.

The stitcher, especially one who attempts relief stitchery, should have an understanding of the nature of spatial relationships in sculpture. To illustrate, random objects sticking out from a flat surface is not good stitchery-in-relief. The success or failure of the total composition depends on the harmony between form itself and the space it invades. That form should *relate* to that space, and it should be defined by it. In other words, the craftsman must learn to discipline the background areas in relief work the way he does form.

Free-standing stitchery is big brother to relief. Here form should predominate. The piece is meant to be seen from every angle, so naturally it should work from every angle. Always keep in mind that when you create a piece of stitchery-in-the-round you are creating a piece of sculpture. A busy surface—intricate embroidery, elaborate textures, distracting colors—won't help if the form itself is not clearly defined.

This book is not an instruction manual. There are already many excellent books available for that. What it is, is a general discussion of stitchery and a selection of pictures designed to give the reader an idea of what's being done by craftsmen in Scandinavia. I hope you will come away from it with a fuller appreciation of the nature of stitchery. And if you are a stitcher, or aspire to be one, I hope your desire after reading this book will be to create objects that are not only beautiful but individual—your own. To imitate is, after all, to miss the point of what I am saying and, more important, to miss the whole point of creative stitchery.

TECHNIQUES OF STITCHERY

Every piece of stitchery requires a plan of sorts. Some craftsmen work from detailed patterns traced onto background fabric, others from only a rough sketch, and others without any guidelines at all. Your method of planning is a personal matter. The important thing is to leave room for experimentation, for impulse, for new design alternatives.

For the beginning student it is often best to start with a pattern. Work out different designs on heavy paper or light tagboard first, then test them out with various fabrics and threads. In other words, *doodle* first with your materials to get a feel for your craft.

STITCHES There are no hard and fast rules for making stitches. Techniques can be altered, styles mixed, and there is always room for the original touch. It is through trial and error that the craftsman discovers how and when to use a certain stitch. Whether, for example, it is feasible to execute a chain stitch with metallic thread; or how a fish-bone stitch done with string will look against coarse burlap. He also learns that every type of stitch has a unique quality—a distinctive look or a particular strength—that makes it especially workable in a specific composition.

Some of the basic embroidery stitches are the running stitch, the back stitch, the blanket stitch, the chain, the cross-stitch, the knot stitch, the overcast, the buttonhole stitch, the darning stitch, the feather stitch, the fish-bone stitch, and the loop stitch. The following are used in appliqué work: the whip stitch, the slip stitch, the running stitch, the blind stitch, the buttonhole, and the cross-stitch. Excellent examples of all of these styles may be found in the picture section of this book.

SLIT TECHNIQUE   In slit, or cut-through, work, one fabric is laid over another, and then cut out to allow the layer underneath to show through. Slit is an excellent method for contrasting colors and textures, or opaque and transparent materials. The "Christmas Stocking" by Ann-Mari Kornerup (see Figure 63) is a simple composition done in the slit style.

PATCHWORK TECHNIQUE   Patchwork is commonly associated with crazy quilts, brightly colored throws, and blankets made of scraps of fabric sewn together. Like slit, which it somewhat resembles, it is eminently suited to contrasting colors, prints, and textures. "The Cross" by Elizabeth Nordstrom (see Figure C-15) is an outstanding example of patchwork.

APPLIQUE   This technique is good for just about any type of composition—collage, high relief, sculpture-in-the-round. Everything from cloth and yarn to buttons, beads, coins, mirrors, nails, and paperclips are workable in appliqué; and materials can be sewed on, glued on, nailed on, or pressed into backgrounds of wax, tar, bonding cement, even clay. You can make an appliqué composition that is changeable, too. A concealed magnet, for example, will hold a metal object to a background, and it can be moved at will. Margaret Hallek uses snaps and zippers in her work so that designs can be altered by opening and closing fasteners (see Figures 89 and 91 through 94). The same designer has achieved a similarly mobile effect by hanging her fabric like a curtain (see Figures 87, 88, and 90). "The Mourners," in Figure 99, is an inventive idea in high relief, and the figures of "Alfred the Strong Man, Isadora, and Mr. Universe" (see Figure 129) are amusing examples of appliqué-in-the-round.

PULLED THREAD   This technique is good for open work and for contrasting textures. There are several methods; one way is to pull random threads completely out of an existing fabric to produce an irregular pattern in the weave. The results can be startling, as you see in "October" by Maiken Berknov (Figure 140). In this work, the designer stretched burlap across a frame of chicken wire and then deliberately changed its prewoven surface. In another variation, illustrated in Figures 138 and 139, threads are pulled, and the remaining ones variously bound or left free to create areas of negative space. In still a third process, shown in Figure 169, threads are pulled from the edges of fabric to create a fringe. The work of Dorthe Buje (seen in Figure C-5) combines all three variations of the pulled-thread style.

LACE-MAKING   Lace is excellent for compositions involving negative and positive space, and it is also used to give the illusion of relief in more or less flat designs. The technique of lace-making is difficult, and nowadays many craftsmen prefer to obtain their lace ready-made rather than take the trouble to learn it. In several areas of Finland and Denmark, however, craftsmen are still actively engaged in lace-making. The result is called *pillow lace,* because of the pillow-like apparatus used in making it. Pillow lace is normally made from very fine, very thin linen thread, and occasionally from cotton (see Figures 146 through 152 for examples of pillow-lace-making).

It is unfortunate that lace-making is regarded by most stitchers as a thing of the past when, quite the contrary, it is a craft rich in untapped resources for contemporary stitchery. For example, the pillow-lace apparatus, enlarged and used with heavy bobbins and thick cord, will produce endless varieties of open, netlike designs. Linen lace of the type used in Finland can be purchased from the Tampella Linen Mills, and a lace pillow, along with an initial supply of bobbins, can be ordered from Rasto and Salomaa for about twelve dollars. *Nyplayksen Harrastajat* and *Nyplayksen Opas,* two books by the lace-makers of Rauma, offer detailed instructions on the lace-making technique and can also be obtained from Rasto and Salomaa. (For further information on ordering materials, see Materials for Further Study).

CROCHETING   This technique is used for compositions in texture, especially high relief. In Figure 166, a design by Inge Larsen-Ledet, tiny crocheted forms project out from a woven surface. Contrasting yarn colors make raised areas more pronounced. Another outstanding example—this time crocheted free-form sculpture—is the ''Birds' Nests'' by Kirsten Dehlholm (see Figure 159).

Rya and other coarse yarns are excellent for work that needs body, such as the stocking caps in Figures 157 and 158. Coarse threads like wool, plastic, or sisal will produce open, netlike textures. The crocheted pieces by Evelyn Noval (see Figures 162 and 163) illustrate what can be done with such materials.

Knitting is also a good technique for relief. The knitted surface is not, however, as open as a crocheted one, and it appears to be less structured. "Brothers Strikker" (Figure 167) is an example of sculpture developed by knitting. Incidentally, Miss Dehlholm knitted this piece with 14-inch needles.

KNOTTING Knotting is perhaps the least explored of all stitchery techniques—and one with unlimited potential. Whereas crocheting and knitting will produce forms with hollow centers, knotting will give you solid forms. Fishermen's and sailors' knots, used for centuries by seamen, are excellent for relief work and sculpture-in-the-round. The seaman knotted forms as bumpers to prevent ships from slapping against their moorings. The stitcher can develop the same knots into disciplined, free-standing sculpture. A simple French-embroidery knot is the basis for the intriguing composition by Kirsten Dehlholm illustrated in Figures 178 and 179.

Rya knotting is usually associated with weaving, but thick, soft rya yarn works very well for stitchery knots, too. Knotted tufts can be tied tightly to make dense forms and clumped together for compositions in bold relief or left to hang loose against a background. Different effects can also be obtained by trimming ends evenly, leaving them ragged, or letting them hang in long shags. Braiding, like knotting, is well suited for contrasting textures and for work in relief and in the round. The technique for making a standard, three-strand braid can be expanded to include up to twenty-one strands of varying colors and textures.

Techniques for knotting are not difficult to learn. A text which is especially rich in ideas for the stitchery craftsman is *The Encyclopedia of Knots and Fancy Rope Work* by Raoul Graumont and John Hensel. A companion book in this series, on weaving, includes a comprehensive discussion of knots, and at the back of this book, there is also a list of yarn suppliers in Scandinavia.

RELIEF AND SCULPTURE   In addition to the methods already covered, there are several other ways to develop relief and sculpture in stitchery. In Figure 181, Lone Brinch has built a wire frame to support the knotted forms in her sculpture; and in "Forar" (Figure 134), fabric is stretched over raised configurations built into a frame. In other examples, notably "The Face" (Figure 79), "Pepperfruit" (Figures 130 through 132), and "White on White" (Figure 133), three-dimensional forms are stuffed or filled with acrylic and foam rubber.

MIXING STYLES   The craftsman who mixes two or more styles in a stitchery composition should keep this thought in mind when he plans his work: too much of only one thing *can* be boring, but too much activity can lead to visual confusion.

Another caution—about "techniquism": creativity in stitchery does not come from simply memorizing complicated techniques. You the craftsman should be master over technique, not its blind slave. You should know *what* it's good for, and *when* and *how* to use it in a composition. And there's absolutely no point in learning a technique if it's not going to be useful—if it doesn't suit *your* type of work. If there's a real need—you have mastered the ones you already use, and your curiosity demands it—then by all means go ahead. But remember never to become like the parrot who is able to mimic words, but doesn't know what they mean, and thus cannot ever use them to his own advantage.

SUMMARY: THE BUSINESS OF WALL HANGINGS

At this moment in Scandinavia and the United States, and in many other countries too, stitchers seem to be single-mindedly pursuing one end: to make wall hangings. Hopefully, the smaller ones are finding their way into private homes. But the large ones need large walls, and so they are being consigned to public and private institutions where, unfortunately, many people will never get to see them. It's just conceivable that if these stitchers continue at their present pace, the world will soon run out of walls on which to hang their hangings!

Despite advanced techniques, new design freedom, the craftsman goes on believing that wall hangings are the only "artistic" way he can express himself. And students are the worst offenders: it is through them that the myth is perpetuated. Meanwhile, back at the studio, dozens of functional projects stand sorely neglected.

There is nothing in the definition of stitchery that demands a wall. In contrast to the perhaps ten minutes of pleasure gotten from looking at a wall hanging, think of the thousands of hours of enjoyment you can get from, say, an embroidered poncho. That stitchery can be worn down the street, to the theater, to a concert, anywhere. And *that* stitchery makes art a living experience.

Stitchery is in its infancy, and the world is hungry for its product. The stitcher needs no longer worry about the stigma attached to "needlecraft." He should be above such concerns because he knows that he can apply the same inventiveness he has used in wall hangings to dozens of functional pieces—stuffed toys, furniture fabric, curtains, room dividers, place mats, tablecloths, quilts, scarves, dresses, capes, neckties, shirts, and, yes, even pillow cases, tea cozies, and doilies. Certainly, this world of ours needs a few more good-looking, useful, everyday items more than it needs another few hundred wall hangings.

C-1. "Apollo X," an assemblage of appliquéd fabrics. By Lars and Gunilla Johanson of Sweden.

C-2. Appliquéd wall ·hanging by a student
(Ateneum, Helsinki, Finland.)

C-3. "Controlling Officer," an assemblage of
appliquéd fabrics combining embroidery.
By Lars and Gunilla Johanson of Sweden.

C-4. "Under Milkwood," appliquéd wall
hanging, machine-sewn, by Agneta Goes of
Sweden.

C-4

C-2

C-3

26

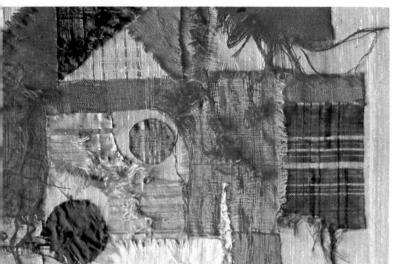

C-5. "Composition," open-work room divider using one variation of the pulled-thread technique. By Dorthe Buje of Denmark.

C-6. Embroidered wall hanging by Eli Marie Johansen of Norway. (Courtesy of Forlaget Bonytt A/S.)

C-7. "Tales" by Ulla Norvell of Sweden. The patches were first knitted and then sewn together into a composition. (Courtesy of Marta Rinde-Ramsback.)

C-8. "The Wonderful Garden of the Persian Shah," by Ann-Cathrine Broome of Sweden. The inspiration for this piece came from a short story entitled "The Silk Carpet" by Yascha Golowanjuk. The designer calls the technique "pearl embroidery" because she includes glass and plastic pearls, artificial flowers, and even jewelry. Materials used also include silk, cotton, fur, and old lace.

C-9. "Figures" by Angela Utbult of Sweden. Wood and copper threads have been appliquéd on the background. (Courtesy of Marta Rinde-Ramsback.)

C-7

C-8

C-9

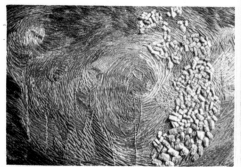

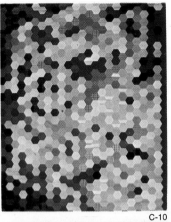

C-10

C-11

C-10. "Blue Meadow," piece using the patchwork technique on cotton. By Elisabeth Osterberg of Sweden. (Courtesy of Marta Rinde-Ramsback.)

C-11. "Lalli's Pasture" by Agneta Goes. It combines silk, cotton, velvet, linen, and metal threads. (Courtesy of Marta Rinde-Ramsback.)

C-12. Appliquéd wall hanging, machine-sewn, by Agneta Goes of Sweden.

C-12

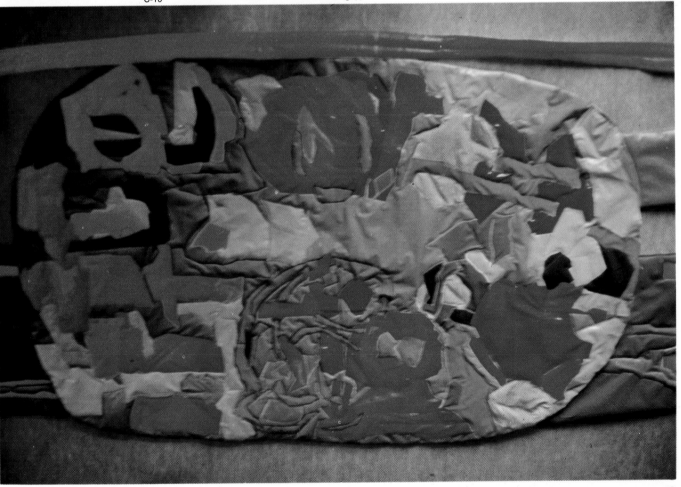

C-13. "Flowering Crown of Thorns," embroidered clerical vestment. By Sonja Hahn-Ekberg of Sweden.

C-14. "Eternity," embroidered clerical vestment. By Sonja Hahn-Ekberg of Sweden.

C-15. "The Cross" by Elizabeth Nordstrom of Sweden. The technique used is patchwork; the materials, silk and old linen sailcloth. (Courtesy of Marta Rinde-Ramsback.)

C-16. Embroidered brooch by Sonja Hahn-Ekberg of Sweden. Mrs. Ekberg begins with a stiff cardboard core and then embroiders over this with linen yarn, silver and gold threads, and small glass beads.

C-17. Embroidered brooch on a core of stiff cardboard. By Sonja Hahn-Ekberg of Sweden.

C-18. Embroidered brooch by Sonja Hahn-Ekberg of Sweden.

C-13

C-14

C-15

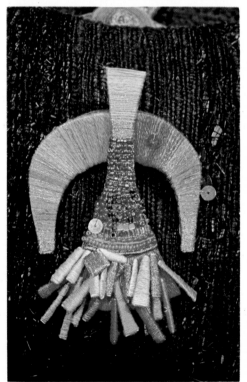
C-16

C-17

C-19. ''Baltazar'' by Marianne Kekonius of Sweden. Cotton appliqué sewn with a machine. (Courtesy of Marta Rinde-Ramsback.)

C-20. Wall hanging by Ulla Hammarsten-McFaul of Sweden. Materials include linen, wood, and silk, plus a rya knotting in the lower right corner.

C-21. ''Homage to Landala'' by Brita Erixon of Sweden. Cotton fabric sewn by machine. (Courtesy of Marta Rinde-Ramsback.)

C-20

C-19

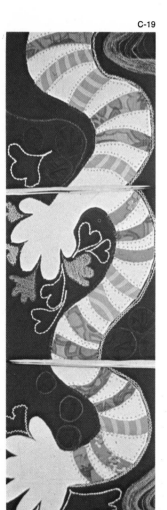

C-21

CROSS-STITCH

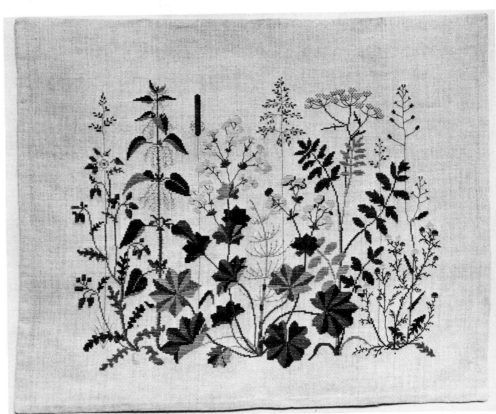

1. "Singers," teapot cover with cotton thread cross-stitched on background of bleached linen. By Gerda Bengtsson of Denmark. (Courtesy of the Danish Handicraft Guild.)

2. "Wild Flowers" cross-stitched with cotton thread on linen background. By Gerda Bengtsson of Denmark. (Courtesy of the Danish Handicraft Guild.)

1

2

3. Karelian festival towel with cross-stitch embroidery. (Courtesy of the National Museum of Finland.)

4. Karelian festival towel with cross-stitch embroidery. (Courtesy of the National Museum of Finland.)

5. ''Nyhavn,'' cross-stitch on bleached linen by Ida Winckler of Denmark. (Courtesy of the Danish Handicraft Guild.)

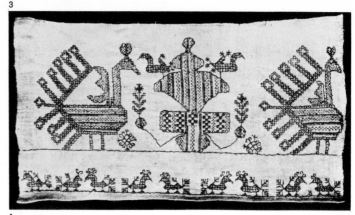

6

6. Embroidered pillow cover, linen thread on cotton, by Elsa-Thordur Hansen of Denmark. (Courtesy of the Danish Handicraft Guild.)

7. Embroidered pillow cover of linen on cotton by Edith Hansen of Denmark. Stitches used are the chain, buttonhole, lazy-daisy, and knot. (Courtesy of the Danish Handicraft Guild.)

7

8. Embroidered wall hanging by Edith Hansen of Denmark. Linen thread is used on unbleached linen. Stitches are chain, buttonhole, lazy-daisy, and knot. (Courtesy of the Danish Handicraft Guild.)

9. Cushion by Edith Hansen of Denmark. Eyelet stitches, counted embroidery, and knots are done with linen thread. (Courtesy of the Danish Handicraft Guild.)

10. Embroidered cushion by Ann-Mari Kornerup of Denmark. It consists of cotton thread over bleached Irish linen with chain, stem, feather, and lazy-daisy stitches. (Courtesy of the Danish Handicraft Guild.)

9

10

11. Linen embroidery, white on white, by Eila Myllyla of Finland. (Courtesy of Ateneum, Helsinki.)

12. Embroidered wall hanging by Hiske Jessen of Denmark. (Courtesy of the Danish Handicraft Guild.)

13. Cushion cover by Bjorn Wiinblad of Denmark. It is linen thread over bleached linen fabric, with chain, coral, buttonhole, herringbone, and knot stitches. (Courtesy of the Danish Handicraft Guild.)

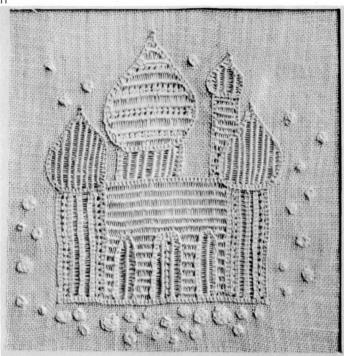

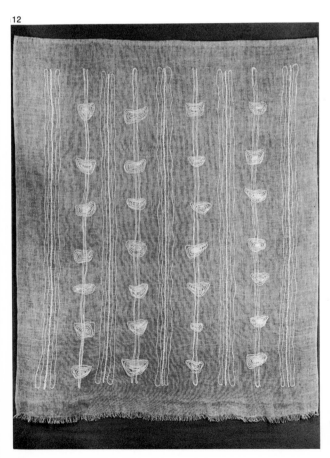

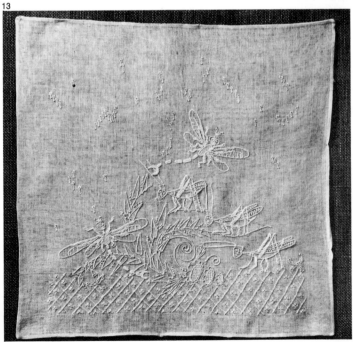

14. "The Newspaper" by Ann-Mari Kornerup of Denmark. Piece combines appliqué with machine zigzag. (Courtesy of the Danish Society of Arts, Crafts, and Industrial Design.)

15. Embroidered wall hanging in silk by Bjorn Wiinblad of Denmark. (Courtesy of the Danish Handicraft Guild.)

16. "Freedom of Speech," three-part embroidered wall hanging by Kaisa Melanton of Sweden. Piece is displayed in the town hall at Vasteras, Sweden.

17. "Samarkand" (detail) by Ann-Mari Kornerup of Denmark. (Courtesy of the Danish Handicraft Guild.)

18. "Samarkand," embroidered wall hanging by Ann-Mari Kornerup of Denmark. (Courtesy of the Danish Handicraft Guild.)

19. "Mantsi," embroidered wall hanging
by Oili Maki of Finland. Silk thread is used
on linen fabric.

20. Detail of large, three-part wall hanging
by Oili Maki of Finland.

19

20

21. ''Sometimes It's Hard to Keep Clean,'' appliquéd and embroidered wall hanging by Kaisa Melanton of Sweden.

22. "To Be, to Feel, to Know, to Dare,"
appliquéd and embroidered theater curtain
by Kaisa Melanton of Sweden.

22

23

24

25

23. "To Be, to Feel, to Know, to Dare" (detail) by Kaisa Melanton of Sweden. The curtain is used in a Stockholm school.

24. "To Be, to Feel, to Know, to Dare" (detail) by Kaisa Melanton of Sweden.

25. "To Be, to Feel, to Know, to Dare" (detail) by Kaisa Melanton of Sweden.

26. "The Long Winter Sleep" by Barbro
Sprinchorn of Sweden. Linen background
and linen thread.

26

28. Embroidered wall hanging by Barbro Sprinchorn of Sweden. (Courtesy of Svenska Slojdforeningen.)

29. Embroidered curtain by Inga-Mi Vannerus of Sweden. (Courtesy of Konstindustriskolan, Goteborg.)

29

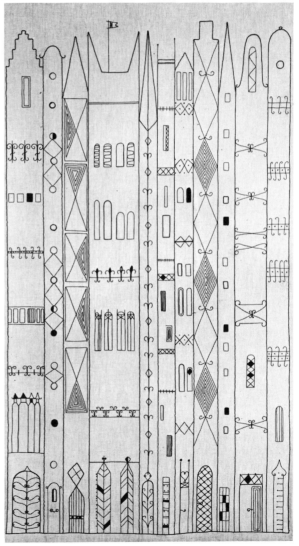

28

30. "Tree of Life" by Clara Salander of Sweden.

31. "The King of Ice and Snow," linen and silk embroidery by Gunilla Sjogren of Sweden.

30

31

32. "Family Album" by Clara Salander
of Sweden.

33. Embroidery with wire and metal attached
to a wood frame. By Clara Salander of
Sweden.

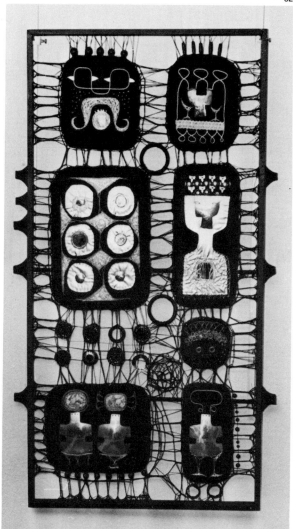

34. "Adam and Eve" by Clara Salander
of Sweden.

35. "François I," embroidery and appliqué
by U-B Emitslof-Dejmo of Sweden.

34

35

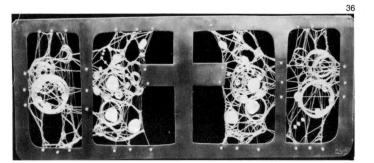

36. Pulpit cloth for church at Stromback, Sweden, using brass, nylon thread, and pearls. By Clara Salander of Sweden.

37. "François II," embroidery and appliqué by U-B Emitslof-Dejmo of Sweden.

38. ''Timglaset,'' embroidery by Ulla
Schumacher-Percy of Sweden. (Courtesy of
Konstindustriskolan, Goteborg.)

39. ''The Boat'' by Ulla Hammarsten-McFaul
of Sweden.

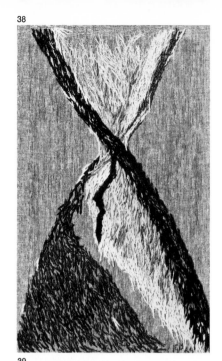

40. "The Lady of Shalott" by Ulla Hammarsten-McFaul of Sweden.

41. "Forbannelsen" by Ulla Hammarsten-McFaul of Sweden.

42. "Sea Floor" by Inger Plangmann of Denmark. Tar yarn, fish net, feather, and linen are used.

43. "Sea Floor" by Jytte Harborsgaard of Denmark uses copper thread, tar yarn, and linen.

44. Combination weaving and embroidery by Maiken Berknov of Denmark. (Courtesy of the Danish Handicraft Guild.)

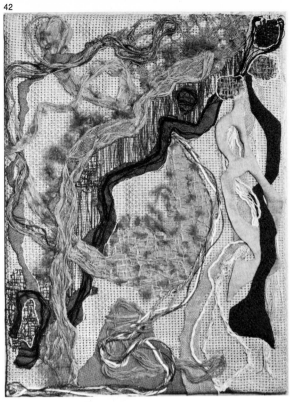
42

43

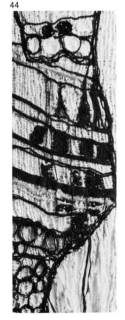
44

45. "Fruit" by Maiken Berknov of Denmark. Cotton, fish net, silk thread, and silk and cotton ribbon are used.

46. "Fruit" (detail) by Maiken Berknov of Denmark.

46

47. "Trifit" by Maiken Berknov of Denmark. Cotton, fish net, linen, silk, and silk ribbon are used.

48. "Trifit" (detail) by Maiken Berknov of Denmark.

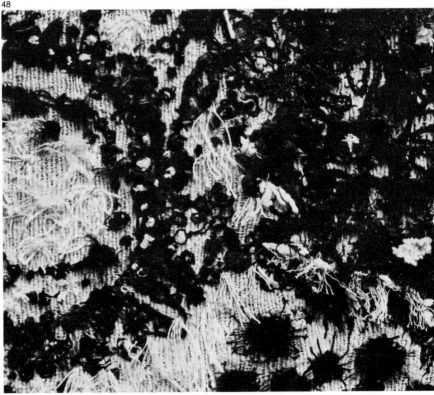

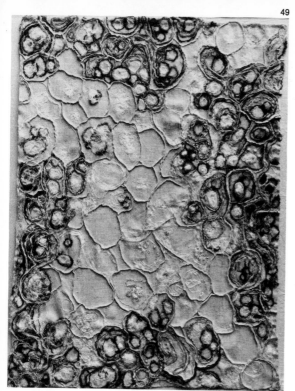

49. "A Lake in Frost" by Maiken Berknov of Denmark. Sisal, mohair, glass beads, and glass fiber are used.

50. "A Lake in Frost" (detail) by Maiken Berknov of Denmark. The relief was gained by gathering the background fabric and stitching it into ridges.

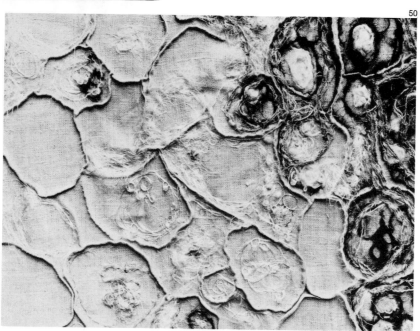

50

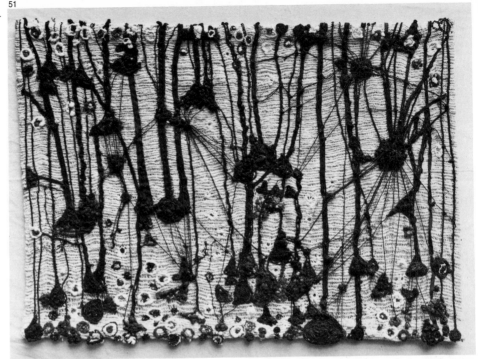

51. "Trees" by Maiken Berknov of Denmark. Cotton, fish net, linen, silk, and silk and cotton ribbon are used.

52. "Trees" (detail) by Maiken Berknov of Denmark.

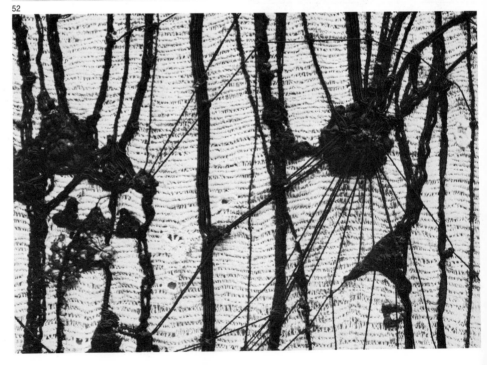

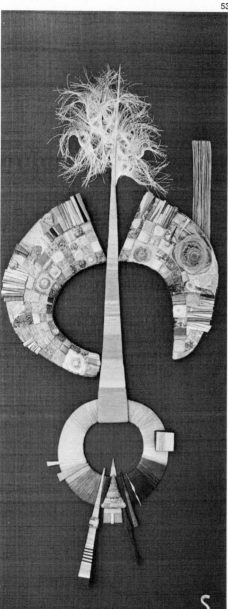

53. "Femme Fatale," stitchery over cardboard core by Sonja Hahn-Ekberg. The "hair" in this design is made with silver and gold thread.

54. "Thread Collage" by Grete Balle of Denmark is done on coarse canvas with wool and linen threads. Some areas are hand-dyed for tones.

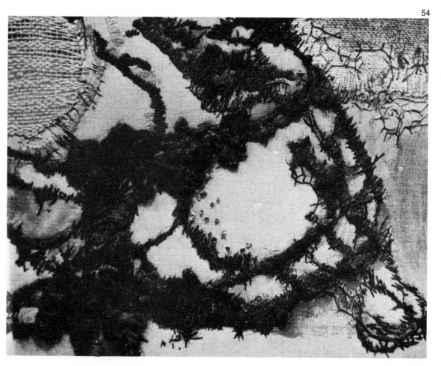

54

55. "Lek Med Garn" by Inger Sarin of Sweden. (Courtesy of Rohsska Museet, Goteborg.)

56. Silk embroidery by Gunilla Sjogren of Sweden.

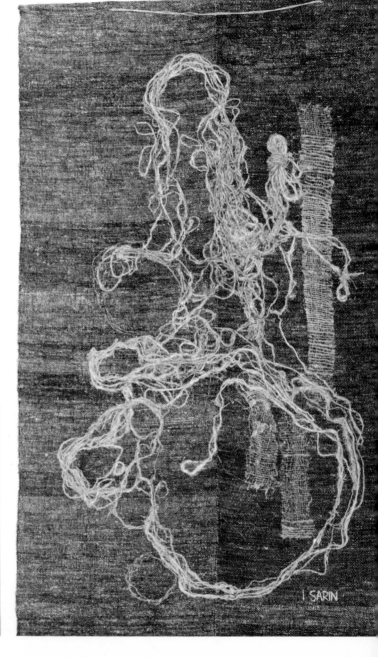

57. Embroidery detail from work by Sten Kauppi of Sweden. (Courtesy of Svenska Slojdforeningen.)

58. Embroidery detail from work by Sten Kauppi of Sweden. (Courtesy of Svenska Slojdforeningen.)

59. Embroidery detail from work by Sten Kauppi of Sweden. (Courtesy of Svenska Slojdforeningen.)

58

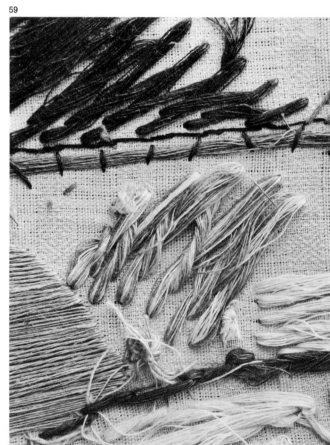

59

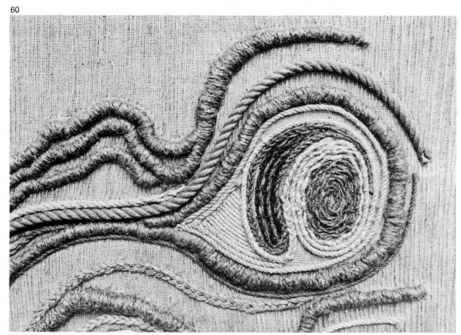

SLIT
AND
APPLIQUE

60. Detail of "Tovvaerk," a rope appliqué by Kirsten Thorsøe of Denmark.

61. "Tovvaerk" (detail) by Kirsten Thorsøe of Denmark.

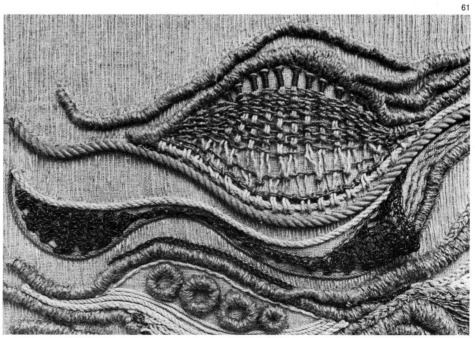

62. Appliqué by Else Marie Jacobsen of Norway.

63. "Christmas Stocking," machine-sewn slit appliqué by Ann-Mari Kornerup of Denmark. (Courtesy of the Danish Handicraft Guild.)

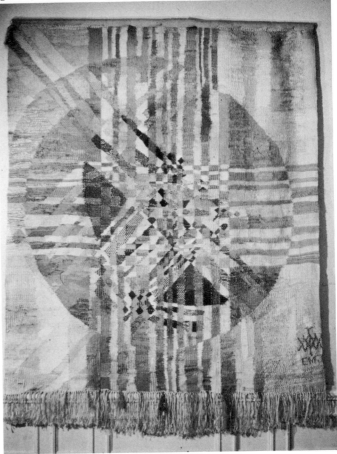

62

63

64. "Covent Garden," appliqué with pearls, mirror glass, and plastic. By Agneta Goes of Sweden.

65. "Metamorfor" appliqué sewn on a machine. By Agneta Goes of Sweden.

66. "Tales," appliqué of silk with threads of silk and metal sewn on a machine. By Asaberg of Sweden. (Courtesy of Marta Rinde-Ramsback.)

67. "Landscape," appliqué sewn on a machine. By Agneta Goes of Sweden.

68. "Butterfly," appliqué of silk, sewn on a machine. By Agneta Goes of Sweden. (Courtesy of Marta Rinde-Ramsback.)

66

67

68

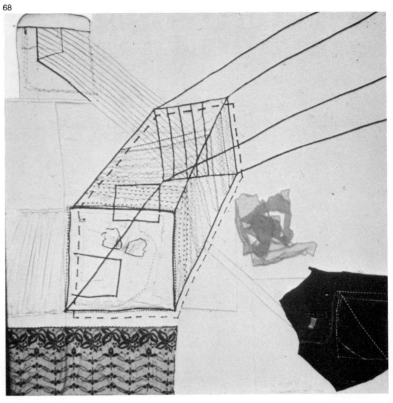

69. "XYZ," appliqué in linen, wool, and cotton sewn on a machine. By Ulla Forsman of Sweden. (Courtesy of Marta Rinde-Ramsback.)

70. "Metafor," appliqué in linen, sewn on a machine. By Sophie De Knoop of Sweden. (Courtesy of Marta Rinde-Ramsback.)

71. "Exterior," appliqué in silk and plastic, sewn on a machine. By Agneta Goes of Sweden. (Courtesy of Marta Rinde-Ramsback.)

69

70

71

72. "Roulette," patchwork with pockets in cotton by Mona Carbe of Sweden. (Courtesy of Marta Rinde-Ramsback.)

73. Silk appliqué with silk embroidery by Bodil Svaboe of Sweden. (Courtesy of Marta Rinde-Ramsback.)

72

73

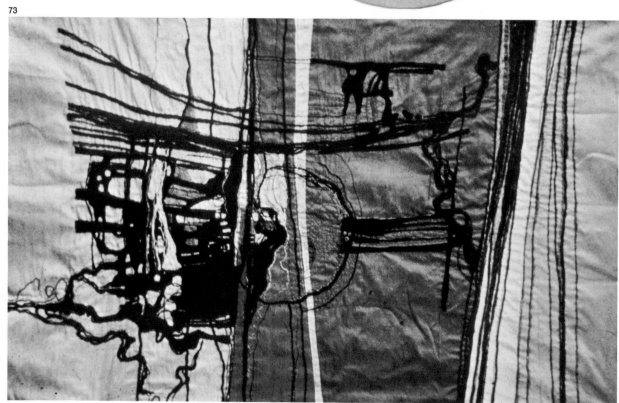

74

74. Appliquéd priest's robe by Gunilla Sjogren of Sweden. Silk fabric appliquéd to wool robe.

75. Priest's robe (detail) by Gunilla Sjogren of Sweden.

76. Appliquéd priest's robe by Gunilla Sjogren of Sweden. Silk pieces appliquéd over wool.

75

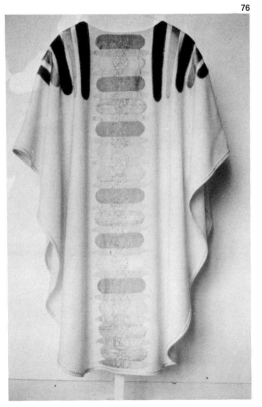

76

77. "Tippe," composition of appliquéd sequins. By Jette Vibeke of Denmark. (Courtesy of the Danish Handicraft Guild.)

78. "Fossil," appliqué by Karin Hellman of Finland. Cotton, linen, wool, and beach stones are sewn with overcast, stem, buttonhole, and cross-stitch.

79. "The Face," by Sophie De Knoop of Sweden. This piece is made in a black, shadow-box frame filled with foam rubber and covered with velvet. The face is also filled. (Courtesy of Marta Rinde-Ramsback.)

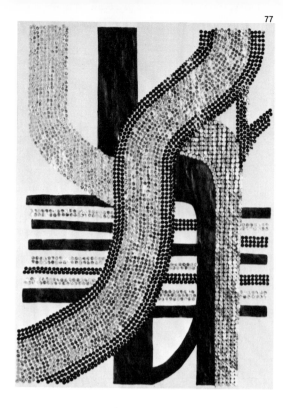

78

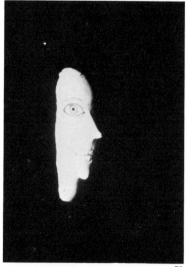

79

80. Machine-stitched appliqué in silk and cotton. By Ellen Malmer and Annette Birch Nielsen of Denmark. (Courtesy of the Danish Handicraft Guild.)

81. "TV Ladies," appliqué in silk by Birgitta Hahn. (Courtesy of the Danish Handicraft Guild.)

80

81

82. "Shewolf" by Lars and Gunilla Johanson of Sweden. (Courtesy of Kollegiet for Sverige—Information.)

83. "Do You Like Oysters?" by Lars and Gunilla Johanson of Sweden. (Courtesy of Kollegiet for Sverige—Information.)

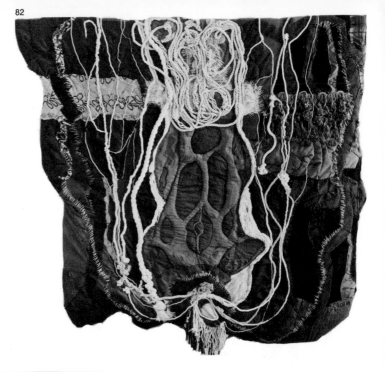

83

84. "Obscurity," appliqué. By Lars and Gunilla Johanson of Sweden. (Courtesy of Kollegiet for Sverige-Information.)

85. Appliqué using glue by Gunvor and Timme Hansen of Denmark. (Courtesy of the Danish Handicraft Guild.)

85

86. "The Dream of Childhood," appliquéd curtain for Kumla, Sweden, prison. By Kaisa Melanton of Sweden. The fabrics used include felt, fiberglass, and silk. The threads include linen and bast.

87. "Changeable Gathers" (variation I) by Margaret Hallek of Sweden. The piece is hung like a curtain, and its composition is changeable. The fabrics include cotton, velvet, and silk.

88. "Changeable Gathers" (variation II) by Margaret Hallek of Sweden.

86

87

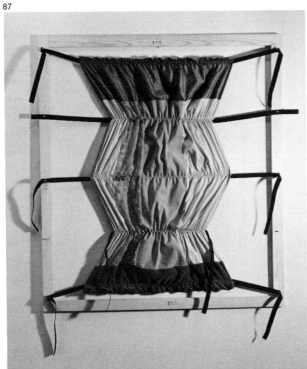

88

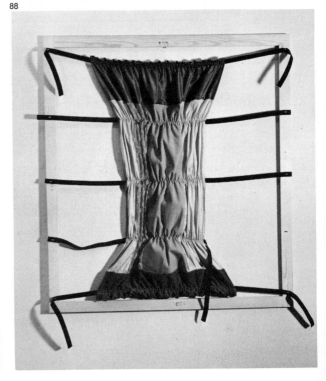

89. "Once Upon a Time," a changeable appliqué using snap fasteners so that the composition can be altered. As the title indicates, it is designed especially for storytelling. Materials include velvet, cotton, silk, and lace. By Margaret Hallek of Sweden.

90. "Changeable Gathers" (variation III) by Margaret Hallek of Sweden.

90

91. "Happy New Year" (variation I), changeable appliqué using zippers. The outside surface is velvet, the inside surfaces are lined with a variety of prints in silk. By Margaret Hallek of Sweden.

92. "Happy New Year" (variation II) by Margaret Hallek of Sweden.

91

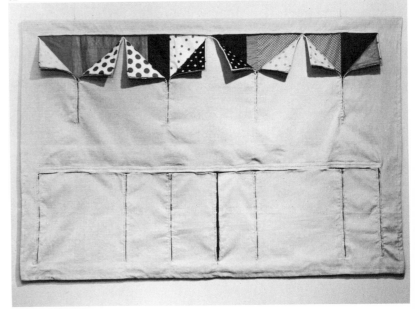

92

93. "Happy New Year" (variation III) by Margaret Hallek of Sweden.

94. "Happy New Year" (variation IV) by Margaret Hallek of Sweden.

95. "The Hanging Gardens of Queen Semiramis" by Ulva Ugerup of Sweden.

96. "Easter" by Ulva Ugerup of Sweden. A fabric background is appliquéd with pearls, buttons, coins, and more fabric.

97. "Thou Art Peter" by Ulva Ugerup of Sweden. The composition is suspended from a coat hanger in front of background fabric.

95

96

97

98. "The Tiger Is Coming" by Ulva Ugerup of Sweden.

99. "The Mourners" by Ulva Ugerup of Sweden. The heads, hands, and feet are filled forms appliquéd against the black background.

100. Cotton application, machine-sewn, by Howard Smith of Finland.

99

100

101. ''Puzzle,'' linen appliquéd with a sewing machine. By Monica Hjelm of Sweden. The square pieces have buttons in order to make the composition changeable. (Courtesy of Marta Rinde-Ramsback.)

102. Cotton application, machine-sewn, by Howard Smith of Finland.

103. Hard-edge cotton application, machine-sewn, by Howard Smith of Finland.

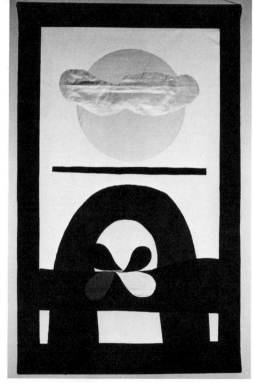

104. "Crow Tree," appliqué and embroidery by Clara Salander of Sweden.

105. Cotton appliqué stretched over wood frame. By Jytte Grindsted of Denmark. (Courtesy of the Danish Handicraft Guild.)

106. ''The Red Square'' by U-B Emitslof-Dejmo of Sweden.

107. ''Energy'' by U-B Emitslof-Dejmo of Sweden.

108. "Klotet och dimmorna II" by Carola
Lind of Sweden. This is a vivid example of
how fabrics can be used in transparency.
(Courtesy of Rohsska Museet, Goteborg.)

109. Appliqué in plastic by Evelyn Noval of Denmark. Within the composition are forms crocheted with plastic threads.

110. Poncho with appliquéd feathers by Birgit Rastrup-Larsen of Denmark. The poncho was woven on a loom, but the feathers were appliquéd by hand.

111. "The Jockey," appliquéd felt, by Birgit Rastrup-Larsen of Denmark.

109

110

111

112. Detail of composition by Maiken Berknov of Denmark using appliquéd coils of metal filings, springs, and electric cord.

113. Appliqué by Britta Penje of Sweden. It is a composition in negative and positive space, with forms cut out of appliquéd fabric. (Courtesy of Svenska Slojdforeningen.)

113

114. ''Sea Flowers'' by Britta Penje of Sweden. (Courtesy of Svenska Slojdforeningen.)

115. Student work. (Courtesy of Ateneum, Helsinki.)

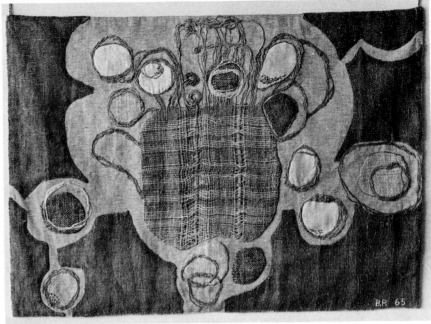

115

116

116. "Collage I" by Karin Hellman of Finland.

117. "Black and White," glued pieces by Karin Hellman of Finland.

118. "Venus of Willendorf" by Karin Hellman of Finland. Materials include linen, velvet, wool, jute, leather, and feathers.

117

118

119. "Girl and Cock" by Karin Hellman of
Finland.

120. "Tragedy" by Karin Hellman of Finland.
Painted cotton, wool, and velvet are glued
on rag strips.

121. Reverse side of "Girl and Cock" by
Karin Hellman of Finland.

119

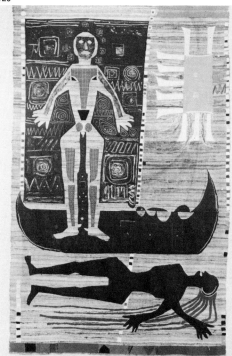

120

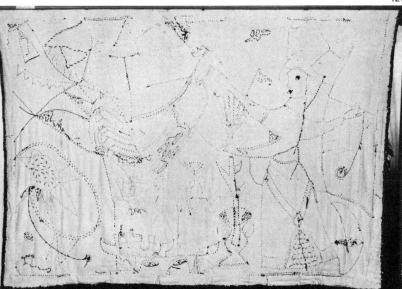

121

122. Patchwork appliqué on pillow by
Elsa-Thordur Hansen of Denmark. (Courtesy
of the Danish Handicraft Guild.)

123. Wall hanging by Margretta Lundberg
of Denmark. (Courtesy of the Danish
Handicraft Guild.)

124. "Children" by Lena Bidstrup of Denmark. Materials include cotton, wood yarn, ribbon, and wire used for the glasses.

125. "Children" (detail) by Lena Bidstrup of Denmark.

125

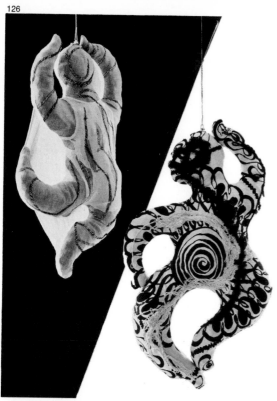

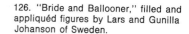

126. "Bride and Ballooner," filled and appliquéd figures by Lars and Gunilla Johanson of Sweden.

127. "Punch Doll," finger puppet with papier-mâché head. By Lars and Gunilla Johanson of Sweden. (Courtesy of Svenska Slojdforeningen.)

128. "Punch Doll," finger puppet with papier-mâché head by Lars and Gunilla Johanson. (Courtesy of Svenska Slojdforeningen.)

129. "Alfred the Strong Man, Isadora, and Mr. Universe," filled and appliquéd figures by Lars and Gunilla Johanson of Sweden.

130. "Pepperfruit" (detail) by Margrethe
Agger of Denmark.

131. "Pepperfruit" (detail) by Margrethe
Agger of Denmark.

132. "Pepperfruit," filled forms by Margrethe
Agger of Denmark.

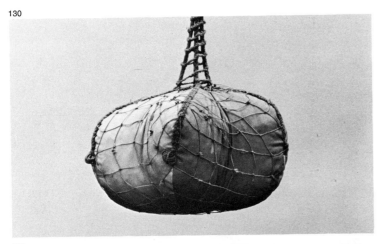

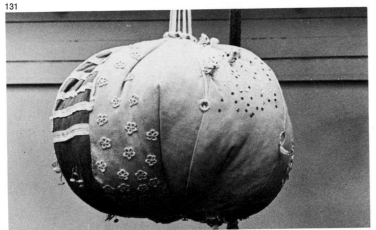

133. "White on White" by Mette Ussing of Denmark. This piece is made from cotton tied in balls and filled with crushed rubber.

134. "Forar" by Ole Reiner of Denmark. A high relief built into a shadow-box frame, covered with fabric, and painted.

134

PULLED THREAD

135. Table doily, bleached-linen background with white linen thread. (Courtesy of the Danish Handicraft Guild.)

136. "Composition" by Lars Andreasson of Sweden. (Courtesy of Konstindustriskolan, Goteborg.)

137. Pulled-thread sampler with bleached linen background and white linen thread. (Courtesy of the Danish Handicraft Guild.)

135

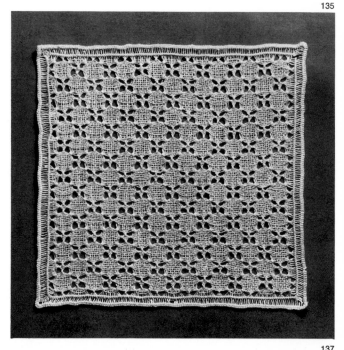

136

137

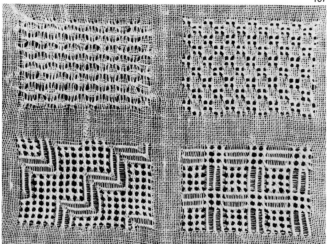

138. Linen curtain by Annette Nielsen of Denmark. Threads are pulled to create windows of open space. (Courtesy of the Danish Handicraft Guild.)

139. "The House," wall hanging in rough linen by Annette Nielsen of Denmark. Threads are pulled or removed to create negative space. (Courtesy of the Danish Handicraft Guild.)

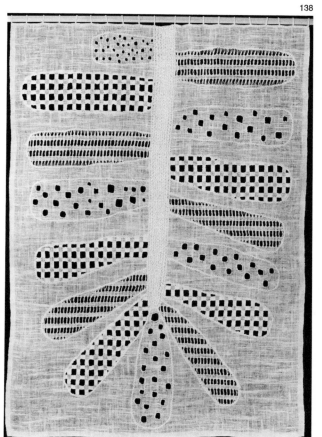

140. "October" by Maiken Berknov of Denmark. The supporting structure for this high relief is chicken wire. Burlap was first stretched over the wire and then appliquéd and embroidered with sisal, tar yarn, and rope.

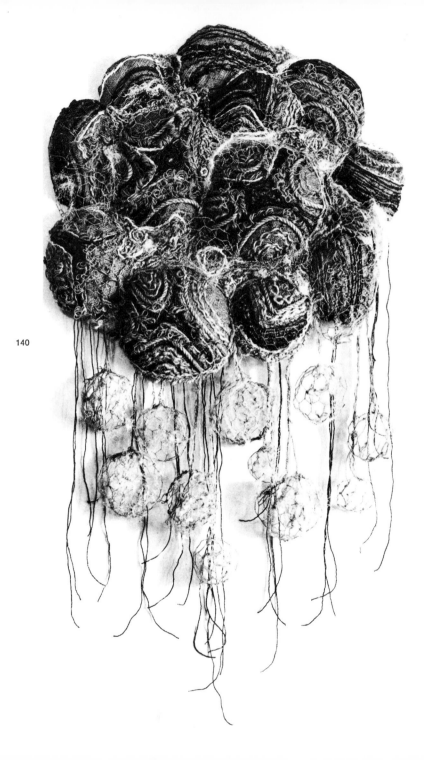

140

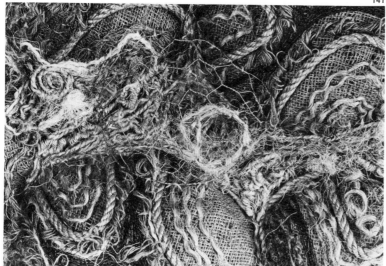

141

141. "October" (detail), Maiken Berknov of Denmark. Occasional threads were pulled from the burlap background to provide a more random texture. One interesting aspect of this piece is that the craftsman did not attempt to hide the chicken wire used to support the relief, but incorporated it into her composition.

142. Detail of embroidery and appliqué in high relief by Maiken Berknov of Denmark. The core structure is chicken wire with burlap, over which is appliquéd thick rope. Embroidery with wire thread frames the holes, made by pulling thread.

143. A second close-up of embroidered wire thread by Maiken Berknov of Denmark.

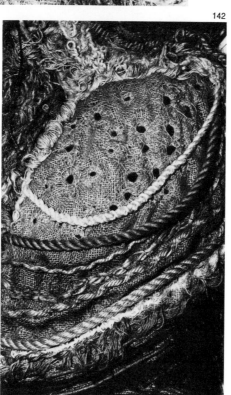

142

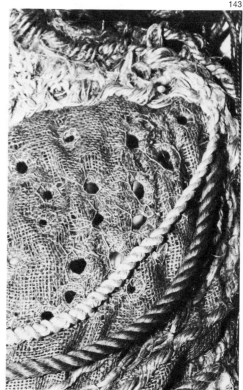

143

144. Curtain by Rolf Middelboe of Denmark.
(Courtesy of the Danish Handicraft Guild.)

145. Pulled-thread curtain (detail) by Rolf
Middelboe of Denmark. (Courtesy of the
Danish Handicraft Guild.)

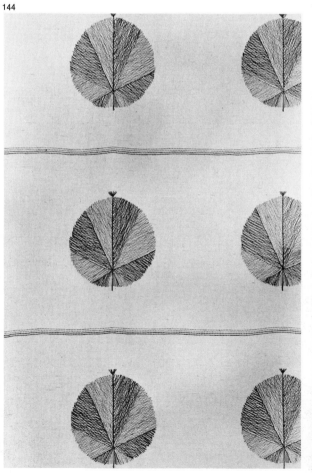

144

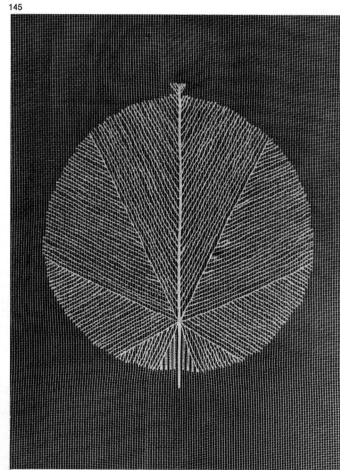

145

146

147

LACE-MAKING

146. Lace-making shown on a homemade lace pillow set into a wicker basket to rotate. (Courtesy of the National Museum of Finland.)

147. Homemade lace pillow tied to a wooden frame. (Courtesy of the National Museum of Finland.)

148. Modern lace pillow (detail). (Courtesy of Handarbetes Vanner and Nordiska Museet, Stockholm.)

149. The lace pillow as used in Rauma. (Courtesy of *Painopiste*, Rauma, Finland.)

148

149

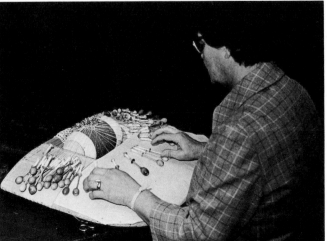

150. Acorn lace made on lace pillow.
(Courtesy of *Nyplayksen Harrastajat.*)

151. Pattern for acorn lace shown in Figure
150. The dots represent the points at which
the pins are set into the pillow. (Courtesy
of *Nyplayksen Harrastajat.*)

152. Detail of one single pillow-lace pattern.
(Courtesy of *Nyplayksen Harrastajat.*)

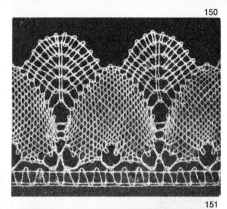

150

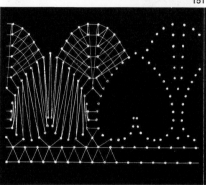

151

152

153. A selection of linen-lace trim from East Gotland, Sweden. (Courtesy of Konstindustriskolan, Goteborg.)

153

154. Open linen-lace work. (Courtesy of
Nyplayksen Harrastajat.)

155. Lace bookmark with pattern. (Courtesy
of *Nyplayksen Harrastajat.*)

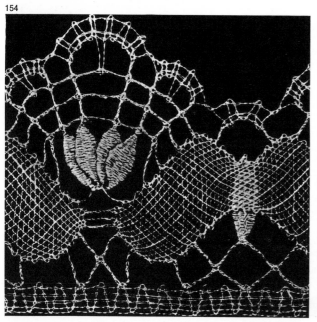

154

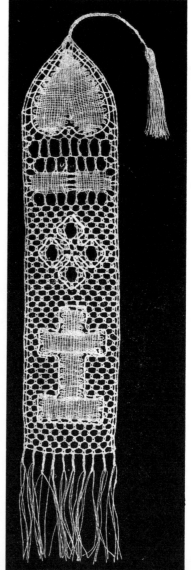

156

CROCHETING

157. Crocheted stocking cap (top view) with three-dimensional forms, made with wool rya yarn. By Birgit Rastrup-Larsen of Denmark.

158. Crocheted stocking cap (front view) by Birgit Rastrup-Larsen of Denmark.

157

158

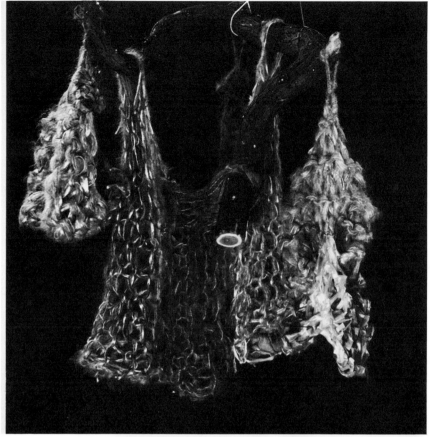

159. "Birds' Nests" by Kirsten Dehlholm of Denmark. The piece hangs suspended from a tree branch. The materials include mohair, bast, and plastic bags cut into strips for crocheting.

160. "Birds' Nests" (detail) by Kirsten Dehlholm of Denmark.

161. "Birds' Nests" (detail) by Kirsten Dehlholm of Denmark.

160   161

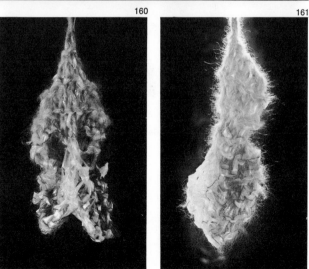

162. Crocheted necklace by Evelyn Noval of Denmark.

163. Crocheted pigtail ties by Evelyn Noval of Denmark.

164. Crocheted necklace by Evelyn Noval of Denmark.

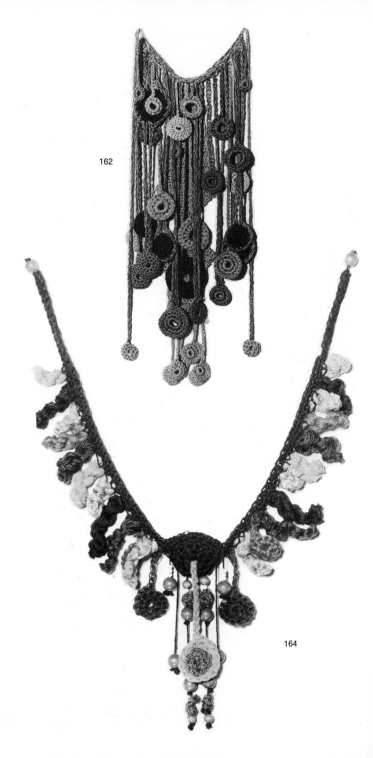

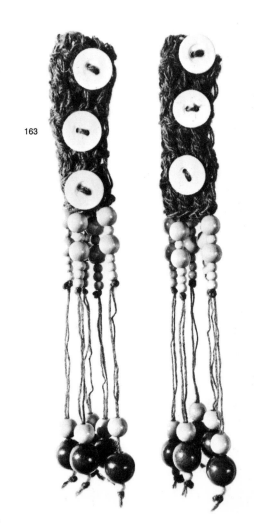

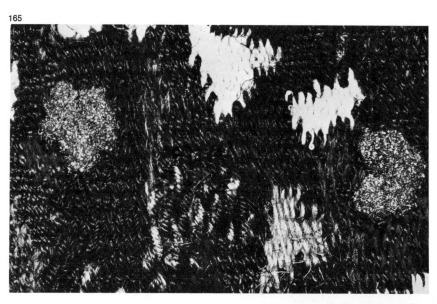

165. Wall hanging (detail) by Inge Larsen-Ledet of Denmark. The two shiny surfaces in the foreground are appliquéd pot cleaners.

166. Wall hanging by Inge Larsen-Ledet of Denmark. Beehive forms are crocheted in relief on a woven surface.

167. "Brothers Strikker" by Kirsten Dehlholm of Denmark. This relief form is knitted from mohair and scrap sailcloth cut into strips.

168. "Brothers Strikker" (detail) by Kirsten Dehlholm of Denmark.

169. "Brothers Strikker" (detail) by Kirsten Dehlholm of Denmark. Threads were pulled to produce a feathered texture on the sail-cloth curls.

168

169

167

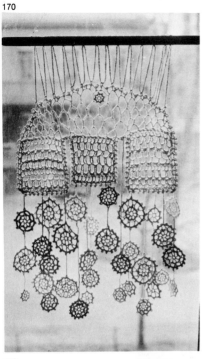

171

172

170. "Joy of Stars in the Light," crocheted window hanging in linen. By Gunilla Sjogren of Sweden.

171. Mini-dress with sculpture (side view) made from filled and machine-sewn stockings. By Kirsten Dehlholm of Denmark.

172. Mini-dress (back view) by Kirsten Dehlholm of Denmark.

173. "Stars on the Lamp," crocheted linen lampshade. By Gunilla Sjogren of Sweden.

174. Experimental mini-dress with sculpture. By Kirsten Dehlholm of Denmark. The round forms are filled with bits of crumpled plastic and tied in place with ribbon. Both mini-dresses are attempts to develop garment sculpture.

173

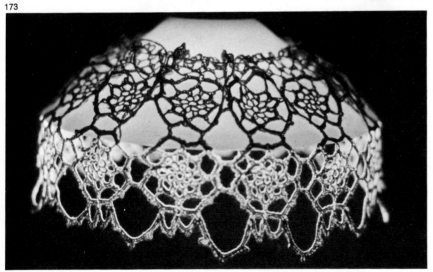

174

KNOTTING

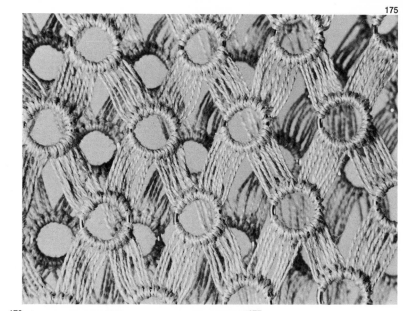

175. Close-up of knotting technique around brass rings. Fabric will be used for a room divider and garments. By Nana Riisager of Denmark.

176. Room divider by Birgitta Mellentin of Denmark. This piece combines knotted sisal, tar yarn, and string with strips of brass tubes.

177. "Tradkuppel I," macramé knotting, by Jette Gemzoe of Denmark.

176

177

178. Bast embroidery with French knots on plaited straw background. By Kirsten Dehlholm of Denmark.

179. Bast embroidery with French knots (detail) by Kirsten Dehlholm of Denmark. Tar yarn was used to embroider the knots against the background. The other material is pigeon feathers.

178

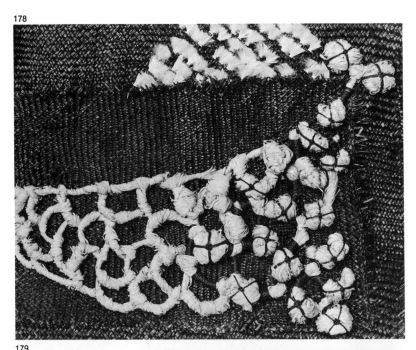

179

180. Window hanging using knotted ribbon, by Bodil Andersen of Denmark. (Courtesy of the Danish Handicraft Guild School.)

181. Knotted bast sculpture by Lone Brinch of Denmark. The material used is synthetic bast, wrapped and knotted around a core of wire.

181

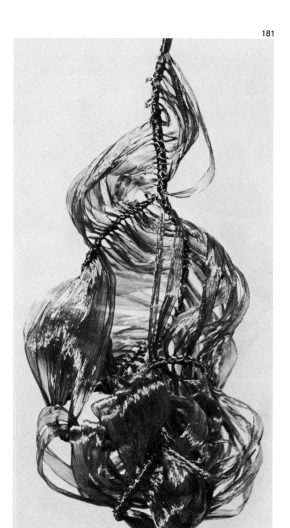

180

LAPP TIN-THREAD EMBROIDERY

182. Modern collar with Lapp tin-thread embroidery. By Gunilla Edvall of Sweden. (Courtesy of Konstindustriskolan, Goteborg.)

183. Tin-thread embroidery by Marianne Nilsson of Swedish Lapland. It is a tradition of the Lapps to embroider with tin or soft pewter thread on traditional costumes. The use of this thread also extends to decorating reindeer harnesses, belts, aprons, handbags, and belt pouches. (Courtesy of Pal-Nils Nilsson.)

184. Lapp tin-thread embroidery used on a blouse front. (Courtesy of Lulea, Sweden, Museum and Pal-Nils Nilsson.)

183

184

185. "Wortles," simple Lapp tools of reindeer horn. Tin is stretched and drawn through the holes to prepare it for embroidery. (Courtesy of Pal-Nils Nilsson.)

186. Here a length of tin thread is being drawn through one of the wortle holes to reduce it to a workable size for embroidery. The trick in drawing the thread is to keep it continually moving at an even pace, because the tin stretches evenly while it is hot. After it has been reduced to the desired thickness, it is spun around a core thread of fine cotton. (Courtesy of Pal-Nils Nilsson and Kristina Wallstrom-Negga, Sweden.)

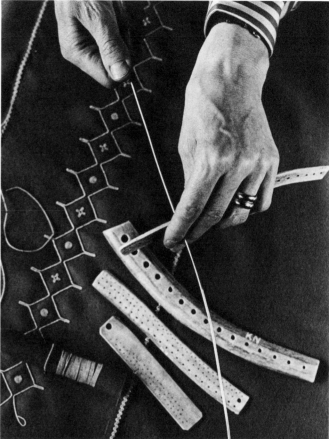

186

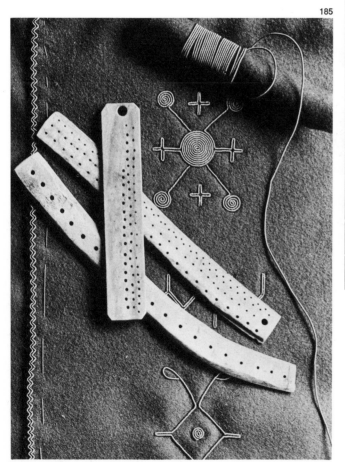

185

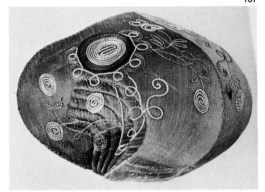

187

EMBROIDERY
FROM THE PAST

187. Embroidered hat from Finland. This is an imitation of the Mary Stuart bonnet, worn by married women in Finland up until about 1850. (Courtesy of the National Museum of Finland.)

188. Top view of embroidered Mary Stuart bonnet. (Courtesy of the National Museum of Finland.)

189. Mary Stuart bonnet with embroidery and lace. (Courtesy of the National Museum of Finland.)

188

189

190. Embroidered carriage seat from town of Gundsømagle in Denmark. (Courtesy of the Danish National Museum and the Danish Handicraft Guild.)

191. "Adam and Eve," embroidered carriage cushion from district of Skane in Sweden. (Courtesy of Nordiska Museet.)

192. "Adam and Eve" (detail). Yarn is wool. (Courtesy of Nordiska Museet.)

190

191

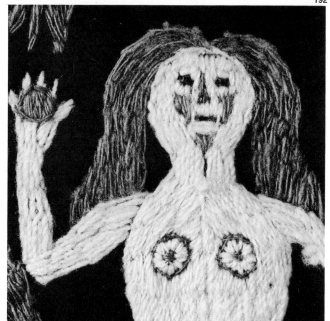

192

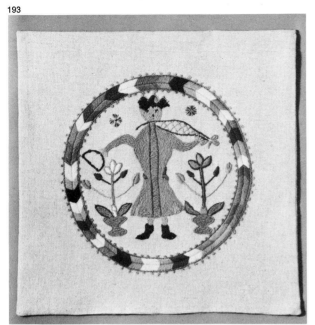

193. "The Husband," embroidered reproduction of eighteenth-century carriage cushion. (Courtesy of the Danish Handicraft Guild.)

194. "Cock Rider's Wife," wool on wool. Piece is based on folk embroidery. (Courtesy of the Danish Handicraft Guild.)

ACKNOWLEDGMENTS

In addition to the many craftsmen who contributed work to this book, I would like to thank the following organizations and individuals who made my research in Scandinavia possible: Maire Walden and the Finnish Press Bureau; Erkki Savolainen and *Look at Finland* magazine; Sinikka Salokorpi and *Avotakka* magazine; the Finnish Design Center and Reino Routamo; the Finnish Society of Crafts and Design and H. O. Gummerus; Ornamo; the National Museum of Finland; and Eila Nevenranta, Matti Timola, and Catharina Kajander—all of Finland. Norsk Design Centrum, Alf Boe, and Janicke Meyer; *Bonytt* magazine; Landsforbundet Norsk Brukskunst; Dr. and Mrs. Peter Anker; and Siri Blackstad—all of Norway. Svenska Slojdforeningen and Birgitta Willen; the Swedish Institute; Anna-Greta Erkner Annerfalk and Kollegiet for Sverige—Information; Claes-Hokan Wihl, his wife, and the staff at Monsanto Scandinavia Ab; *Sweden Now* magazine; Pal-Nils Nilsson; Hemslojdforbundet for Sverige; Konstindustriskolan, Goteborg, and Marta Rinde-Ramsback; Nordiska Museet, Stockholm, Historiska Museet, Stockholm; *Forum* magazine; and the Form Design Center in Malmo— all of Sweden. The Danish Society of Arts, Crafts, and Industrial Design, and Aksel Dahl; the Danish Handicraft Guild and Gertie Wandel and Hanne Zahle; Den Permanente and Mrs. Ole Wanscher; the Royal Danish Ministry for Foreign Affairs Press Office; *Mobilia* magazine; and Ove Hector Nielsen, John Allpass, Kirsten Dehlholm, Inge Kraus, Birgit Rastrup-Larsen, and Mr. and Mrs. Kaj Larsen; all of Denmark.

For travel arrangements, I would like to thank: the Finnish Travel Association and Mrs. Bengt Pihlstrom; Finnair; Oy Finnlines Ab; the Finnish Steamship Company; Bore Lines Ab; the Foreign Ministry of Norway; the Norwegian State Railway; Scandinavian Airlines System; the Swedish State Railway; Swedish American Line; the Danish State Railway; the Royal Danish Ministry for Foreign Affairs; and the United Steamship Company of Denmark.

I would like to thank the following photographers and agencies who have work included in this volume: Ilmari Kostiainen; V. T. Serelius; Tyyni Vahter; Mrs. Koskinen Painopiste; Nousiainen; A. Fethulla; Linnovaara; Martti I. Jaatinen; and Valok. A. Lindell—all of Finland. *Bonytt* magazine, Norway. Pal-Nils Nilsson/Tio; Sten Didrik Bellander/Tio; Tre Fotografer Ab; Ulf Sjostedt; Marta Rinde-Ramsback; Nordiska Museet; Sundahl; Gustav Hansson; H. M. Alexandersson; and Gallerie Blanche—all of Sweden. Ove Hector Nielsen; Mathias Foto; Lilian Bolvinkel; Jonals Foto; Bent Hassing; Struwing Foto; and Carl Rasmussen—all of Denmark.

MATERIALS FOR FURTHER STUDY

The following books and periodicals may be ordered directly from their publishers in Europe and the United States:

otiteollisuus (periodical), emppelikatu 15-A, Helsinki nland.

lila, Aino, Etupistokirjonta, WSOY, orvoo, Finland (1951).

min Kasin (periodical), etalahdenranta 13, Helsinki, Finland.

enij-Ollila, Karjalan kirjonta, WSOY, orvoo, Finland (1951).

ahter, Tyyni, and Laila Karttunen, rjottuja peittoja, Suomalaisen rjallisuuden Seura, Helsinki, nland (1952).

orsk Husflid (periodical), Ø Slottsgate Oslo 1, Norway.

orsk Kunsthandverk, Bonytt Publishing o., Bygdoy Alle 9, Oslo 2, Norway.

rum (periodical), Box 7047, ockholm 7, Sweden.

eiljer, Agnes, Textila Skatter i pala Domkyra, Almqvist & Wiksell, oteborg, Sweden.

emslojden (periodical), Brannkyr-agatan 117, Stockholm, Sweden.

len, Anna-Maja, Swedish Peasant ostumes, Nordiska useet, Stockholm, Sweden.

engtsson, Gerda, Cross-stitch nbroidery (2 vols.), Danish Handicraft Guild, Vimmelskaftet 38, Copenhagen K, Denmark.

Christmas Cross-stitch, Danish Handicraft Guild, Vimmelskaftet 38, Copenhagen K, Denmark.

Dansk Kunsthaandvaerk (periodical), Bredgade 58, 1260 Copenhagen K, Denmark.

Fangel, Esther, Pulled Thread Work (2 vols.), Danish Handicraft Guild, Vimmelskaftet 38, Copenhagen K, Denmark.

Haandarbejdets Fremme (periodical), Danish Handicraft Guild, Vimmelskaftet 38, Copenhagen K, Denmark.

Holbein Work, Danish Handicraft Guild, Vimmelskaftet 38, Copenhagen K, Denmark.

Mobilia (periodical), Snekkersten, Denmark.

Basic Stitches for Creative Stitchery (wall chart), Educational Division, Lily Mills, Shelby, N.C.

Craft Horizons (periodical), American Craftsmen's Council, 44 W. 53 St., New York, N.Y. 10001.

Dictionary of Embroidery Stitches, Woman's Day, Box 1000, Dept. WDL, Greenwich, Conn. 06830 (1961).

Dillmont, Therese, The Encyclopedia of Needlework, D.M.C. Publication.

Grant, Bruce, Leather Braiding, Cornell Maritime Press, Cambridge, Md. 21613.

Graumont & Wenstrom, Encyclopedia of Knots and Fancy Rope Work, Cornell Maritime Press, Cambridge, Md. 21613.

—————, Fishermen's Knots and Nets, Cornell Maritime Press, Cambridge, Md. 21613.

Handweaver and Craftsman (periodical), 246 Fifth Ave., New York, N.Y. 10001.

Hartung, Rolf, Creative Textile Design, Van Nostrand Reinhold Co., 450 W. 33 St., New York, N.Y. 10001.

Harvey, Virginia I., Macramé: the Art of Creative Knotting, Van Nostrand Reinhold Co., 450 W. 33 St., New York, N.Y. 10001.

Karasz, Mariska, Adventures in Stitches, Funk & Wagnalls, 380 Madison Ave., New York, N.Y.

King, Bucky, Creative Canvas Embroidery, Hearthside Press, 381 Park Ave. S., New York, N.Y.

Krevitsky, Nik, Stitchery, Van Nostrand Reinhold Co., 450 W. 33 St., New York, N.Y. 10001.

One Hundred Embroidery Stitches, no. 150, Coats & Clark Sales Corp., 430 Park Ave., New York, N.Y. 10022.

Schuette, Marie, and Sigrid Muller-Christensen, The Art of Embroidery, Frederick A. Praeger, 111 Fourth Ave., New York, N.Y.

Butler, Anne, Teaching Children Embroidery, Studio Vista, London, England.

Thomas, Mary, Dictionary of Embroidery Stitches, Hodder & Stoughton, London, England.

Yarns, thread, and fabric may be obtained from the following Scandinavian mail-order firms:

Helmi Vuorelma Oy, Lahti, Finland.
Kotivilla Oy, Jarvela, Finland

Monsanto Scandinavia Ab, Eriksgatan 32-B, Helsinki, Finland
Neovius Oy, Munkkisaarenkatu 2, Helsinki 15, Finland
Rasto and Salomaa, Isokirkko Katu 7, Rauma, Finland
Tampella Linen Mills, Tampere, Finland
Vokki Oy, Vainamoisenkatu 31-B, Helsinki 10, Finland

Husfliden (the Norwegian Home Arts Association), Møllergate 4, Oslo, Norway

Aktiebolaget Nordiska Kompaniet, Box 7159, Stockholm 7, Sweden
Hemslojdforbundet for Sverige, Sturegatan 29, Stockholm, Sweden

CUM, Rømersgade 5, Copenhagen K, Denmark
The Danish Handicraft Guild, Vimmelskaftet 38, Copenhagen K, Denmark
Julius Koch, Norrebrogade 52, Copenhagen, Denmark
Tomtex, Tordenskjoldsgade 28, 1055, Copenhagen K, Denmark

The following Scandinavian textile schools offer courses in stitchery:

Ateneum, Railway Square, Helsinki 10, Finland
Fredrika Wetterhoffin Kotiteollisuusopettajaopisto, Hameenlinna, Finland

Statens Handverks og Kunstindustriskole, Ullevalsvejen 5, Oslo 1, Norway
Statens Kunstindustriskole, Bergen, Norway
Statens Laererskole i Forming, Cort Adelersgt. 33, Oslo, Norway

Konstfackskolan, Valhallavegen 191, Stockholm, Sweden
Konstindustriskolan, Kristinelundsgatan 6-8, Goteborg C, Sweden
Textilinstitutet, Boras, Sweden

Kunsthaandvaerkskole, Copenhagen, Denmark
Danish Handicraft Guild School, Bredgade 77, Copenhagen K, Denmark

Scandinavian design and handicraft societies and exhibitions:

The Finnish Design Center, Kasarminkatu 19, Helsinki, Finland
The Finnish Society of Crafts and Design, Unionkatu 30, Helsinki 10, Finland
Ornamo, Ainonkatu 3, Helsinki 10, Finland

Landsforbundet Norsk Brukskunst, Uranienborgvejen 2, Oslo 1, Norway
Norsk Design Centrum, Drammensvejen 40, Oslo 2, Norway

The National Association of Swedish Handicraft Societies, Mimervagen 8, Djursholm 2, Sweden

Svenska Slojdforeningen, Nybrogatan 7, Box 7047, Stockholm 7, Sweden

The Danish Handicraft Guild, Vimmelskaftet 38, Copenhagen K, Denmark
The Danish Society of Arts, Crafts, and Industrial Design, Bredgade 58, 1260 Copenhagen K, Denmark
Den Permanente, Vesterport, Copenhagen, Denmark